Bobish

Bobish

Magdalena Ball

PUNCHER & WATTMANN

First published in 2023
Published by Puncher and Wattmann
PO Box 279
Waratah NSW 2298

https://www.puncherandwattmann.com
web@puncherandwattmann.com

ISBN   9781922571601

Cover design by Miranda Douglas, Image: "Author's own photo of Rebecca Lieberman, colourised by Jamil Khann"
Typesetting by Morgan Arnett
Printed by Lightning Source International

A catalogue record for this work is available from the National Library of Australia

NATIONAL LIBRARY OF AUSTRALIA

Contents

Fish Smoker

Beyond the Pale

The Body is an Instrument

Tikkun Olam

Arrival

A Voice to Shatter Glass

Every object has its own
resonant frequency
run a finger along the rim: *ghost hum.*

People lined up at her door
money in closed fists, ready to hear secrets
wrapped in a soothing voice
break the glass.

They came in secret
tea leaves, a gilt-rimmed cup
left with something other than answers
it was not that kind of fortune.

She hummed, a single note amplified
working through the cavity of the mouth
the pharynx, stretched along the larynx,
a portal

carrying sound
mechanical waves move
through gas, liquid, solids
through the medium of time.

Press your ear against the table now
and it's there still
carrying energy outward
from the hallway
of a cramped apartment
smelling of damp clothing
and barley soup

into the streets
into the future
rushing pushing
struggling, shattering
air, water, glass,
irrupting into
the impossible present.

Footprints

She kept her head low
 left few footprints.
 There weren't many traces.

Given the dates
 we can work out what's possible
 if you study the evidence, scant as it is.

Why go so far
 leave behind everything
 mother, father, siblings, home
  forever
 time being what it was
 back then.

Why so many that year
 arriving with the same look
  tired, lost, fearful in sepia
  clutching worn leather bags
   a different migration
   to my own
   but everything is connected.

I wanted to know what it felt like
 and you, Bobish
  you needed to tell me
 even after so many years

 from the relative comfort
of your clean bones
and hidden grave.

The Pale of Settlement

In Imperial Russia
from 1791 to 1917
it was forbidden for Jews
to live beyond The Pale of Settlement.

The Pale contained
the uncivilised, reprehensible
not-really-Russian
banished from the interior.

The original Pale
was designed to keep out
the unpredictable, unwashed Irish.

A strip of land stretching
from Dundalk in Louth
to Daley in Dublin
subject to the English King.

From *palus*, meaning fenced
as in paling fence
a boundary, ring bound.

Separate cultures both forged
from the pressure of
exclusion
struggling against
invisible
lines of demarcation.

She could have gone to Ireland
instead of America
there was family there
so she heard.

There could have been cousins
anywhere, scattered from
sacred homelands

lost tribes, lost family
diaspora of the unwanted
reaching across oceans
and time,
Pale to Pale.

Two kopeks

Seven of them   one room
        grandparents crouched   small alcove below
                broken stove   no daylight.

It was not always
        the winter before   heating   space   a piano
              nimble fingers   unscarred   played in waning light
                  curtains blowing
                      two kopeks in her pocket   for sweets.

The piano burned   in the first pogrom
        no one wanted   that music
              she could no longer   remember   the notes.

Seven hours they   hid in the gap
        fear pungent   as rotting fruit
              gunshot for hours   windows shattering
              hands over the baby's mouth.

They knew then   they would have to go
        only how
              who stays   who goes
              passports can take   months
                    cost   more   than they have

her grandparents   would not have
              survived
          the long journey   steerage
              her parents would   have to   join later
        when she could   send money *gelt*
           order   tickets   her cousins
              had already gone

    promises rained   onto the steamship
           she could not see
      from where she   huddled
for days   she heard those words
             falling   in her head
        like the sound of   gunshot
             shattering windows.

The Black Hundreds

No one remembers anything
or if they remember
they don't want to talk.

You start with a clue. A phrase.
Something resonant.
In this case, *The Black Hundreds*
whispered silently.

There were rumbles at first
the odd beating
break-through bleeding
neighbour against neighbour.

Antisocial, anti-liberal
antisemite: monarchists
knives, knuckledusters, flags
devotion to the Tsar
House of Romanov
church and motherland.

Dry, metallic, caustic
plates falling off the sidebar
scrape of shoes on the tiles
two grooves in the dirt
where they dragged her auntie.

Brutal signs were everywhere
blood, skin, broken bodies
lintel hanging off windows.

Her mother gave her a bag of coins
the brass samovar, told her to pack
quickly.

You didn't need tea leaves
to read what was coming.

Taken with Time

She knew the drill
it was as familiar as sleep

        the worn trajectory of terror
        voices in the distance, banging, barking

            the doppler as they moved closer
            sound increasing in pitch

                like a freight train of atrocities.
                We needn't speak of it

                    it happened, it was in the past
                    she ran, closing her eyes: *don't look back.*

Philology

Her grandparents were forced
　　　to take last names.

How to choose
　　　occupation, toponym
　　　personal qualities, lineage?

Her mother changed her first name
　　　they all did.

Memory rewrote the record
　　　transition into history.

Sources are unreliable
untruths, inaccuracies
　　　they did not want to be discovered.

Names can be used against you
　　　signifiers, identifiers.

Every encounter begins
　　　with the same question:
　　　　　What is your name?

She made one up. Small enough to fit
　　　in a box on a form. Small enough to cup
　　　　　in her hands, to hide inside.
　　　Rivka to Rebecca
　　　　　Rebecca to Beckie.

Her family did not take a name
until they were compelled
    threats of disenfranchisement
      promises of freedom.

First they were forced into the Pale
    tagged, delineated
      then they were expelled.

The threats were carried out
    the promises weren't.

She left everything behind
    except her new name.
      Her surname meant beloved.

Her given name meant
    "bound", "tied", as in, to the earth.

She was unbound, set adrift
    could not find her way back
      there were no maps that led to home.

Even the name of her country changed
    shifted, ceased to exist
      was destroyed
        denied
      but she survived.

Double Migrant

Before she left the largest
       ghetto in the world
             a small woman on a big ship
                  she was already a migrant

                     in the margins of legality
             crouching in the space
       between integration
   and segregation
watching, waiting.

After the Partition

Her father was a Polish-Lithuanian
            merchant
travelling back and forth
            along the Silk Road
heady spices, perfumes, furs, textiles
            whatever people wanted to buy.

Craggy borders against the Baltic Sea
Poland, Lithuania, Latvia, Belarus
carved up and served like brisket
to Russia and Prussia.

After the partition
            he became Russian.

This was not a rapid process
he knew the illusion
of nationality

no matter the name
            Poland, Russia, Belarus, Lithuania
the one constant
            they did not belong.

Arriving in Moscow
banished from the interior
penned in, career cancelled.

Under such pressure
        something woke in him
forcing a transformation.

He would not leave again
no matter what
until everyone else was safe.

Her mother's hair was a frizzy halo
        golden brown beneath a floral kerchief
scent of violets just below perception,
        when neighbours became enemies
the horse fell down in the street
        nothing felt solid enough
        to hold them in place.

Ocean Mandala

Solitude was the feedback loop
she sailed in on.

Every shade of blue reduced, saturated
intensified.

Her eyes became a kaleidoscope
spiralling with the water, refracted

through tears she kept from falling
as the boat steamed towards a destination

imagined and unknown. She was younger
than she looked and she looked like a child.

The steamship was so cramped she claimed
the space beneath her feet just to breathe.

Do I look sick in the eyes?
The sky and the ocean reflected one another

polarised light roiled with the boat.
She swallowed her sickness.

Sickness was not allowed so she kept
her head up, straightened narrow shoulders.

When the boat docked, the city opened from
the deck in blue cobwebs, spirals, tunnels

an interconnected pattern she would learn
to understand. There were so many people

it took three days to disembark. She had been
promised a house, a job, food.

Dizzy, she grabbed the rail for balance.
When she earned enough she would

send a ticket for her parents
if she could find them again.

In the meantime, memory was Prussian Blue
a cyanotype carried like ghostly love.

The Lost Sister

There is evidence to suggest it,
though no one knows.

No diary entries of late-night gossip
or family get togethers
no letters on parchment paper
written by candlelight
after her husband went to bed.

The journey was arduous
anything could have happened.

We know they were guilty of poverty
detained under
a burden of persecution
searching for a new life.

All notes were written in invisible ink
in the solitude of the mind
the shadow self, lamplit.

The other self was tattered, unkempt
verklempt.

She might have covered the younger girl
with her coat, saved her the best scraps
but still she disappeared.

There were so many diseases on the boat:
cholera, the yellow cup-shaped crusts of Favus
Tuberculosis, or worse of all, Trachoma
which could get you sent back
blind, groping for a home that no longer existed
every horror you ran from multiplied.

Guide to the United States for the Jewish Immigrant

The Hebrew Sheltering and Immigrant Aid Society
is open day and night. (On the boat's lower deck
above the closed hold it was impossible to know
if it was day or night – no light entered.)

Immigrant Jews should go exclusively
to this Society for information
otherwise they are likely to be swindled.
(The trip was 70 rubles – all she had –
there was nothing left to swindle.)

Immigrants may use the Society
as a forwarding address for letters.
(No one wrote – they could not.)

A physician and a nurse
are in attendance.
(Illness is forbidden
if you're marked as sick
you will be sent back.)

Prayers take place
at the synagogue
three times a day.
(She was done praying.)

The Clara de Hirsch Home
for Immigrant Girls meets
immigrant women and girls at Ellis Island.
(She was fourteen. Was she a girl or a woman?
Would she ever be safe?)

America is a land of opportunities.
If you work faithfully
you will have many chances
(She clutched a tattered book
shared in secret, carried
across the Atlantic,
and wondered how one might
work unfaithfully?)

Mother of Exiles

She closed one eye and breathed in, swapped to the other, wiping the crusts with dirty fingers then drew back.

The air was fetid, but a tiny breath like hope filtered in as the steerage doors opened.

She didn't know what to expect though there were a thousand lines in her head, a thousand images she'd taken to bed with her every night while she listened, awake and asleep and neither, for horse hooves, fists against the door, her mother's high-pitched wail.

She hoped her parents might have escaped somehow, in an alternate reality, the piano in her memory, already firewood before she left, still played songs of New York in springtime with gilt cobblestones, where light broke slowly against her face emerging from the boat.

She had already written to them, five hidden letters to send when she was safe, if she ever was safe. Many more in her head, still to be put onto paper.

She might have left sooner or later, or never, living and dying where she belonged or never belonged and what is belonging anyway she wondered, moving so slowly in a mass of bodies that it was like standing still.

Tired, cold, but breathing something like a future, she looked up, and saw the lady, blue-green copper-bound mother of exiles, not her mother.

She swallowed that thought and kept on walking though her legs were so heavy they felt as though they could not move one more step.

She heard the words not spoken, from the pedestal, *you are sea-washed, you are here.*

Empire Erased

It was over in an hour
a thousand people in an hour.

Who dared count the weary passengers
disembarking from the cramped steerage
Zwischendeck
lips cracked from sea salt.

Bribes, promises
as many illicit exchanges
as there were people
as there were dreams
not so much of something better
but of safety.

Someone has to survive to pass on the story.

They kept on moving, checkpoint to checkpoint
fingers probing hair (*no lice*), clothing (*old, stiff*)
cough, lean forward, raise arms, keep going.

An empire was erased
just like that.
She would never go back.

There were people left behind of course
in the ghetto of her youth: the *shtetl*
writing names in the air with a finger

waiting for her to send
a handful of prepaid tickets

if the streets really were paved with gold.

Words were cobblestones
beneath her feet
thirty one questions in a language
she didn't speak: name, age, sex
nationality, health, how much money
was in her pocket, *was she dangerous?*

At five feet tall with arms like matchsticks
hooded eyes concealing more pain
than a malnourished body should
be able to hold, how do you answer?

She tried, and failed, to forget
her mother's wet eyes
her father's hastily gathered bag of coins
cousins, uncles.

Of course they existed somewhere
but who knows what happened to them
their sacrifices, their losses.

They're gone. Were they ever there?
Keep up the pace.

She tried to speak
but the words didn't fit her mouth
there were no papers, only a brown tag pinned
to the shoulder, containing a number
like a price you might put on cattle.

She wasn't for sale
her number wasn't up this time.

Small Woman with a Big Bag

After the voyage
everywhere filthy, stinking
the smell might never wash off

she wanted nothing more
than to get rid of the thing, though it was
the whole of her life: her father's coins
the metal tea samovar with which she hoped
to earn her living reading the future

a place she no longer believed in
clothing she now described
as old world rags
and black tea, wrapped tightly
in her undergarments.

How else would she live?

She saved all the money
she made reading leaves
people secretly lining up at her door.

It was never legal, though
even her own body was illegal.
She was the wrong type
wrong religion, cheekbones too high
skin too olive, chin too small, her lips
her blood, everything about her was bad.

People spat at her in the street
men on horses slowed down to leer.
She was fourteen, almost a woman.
It was leave or die.

She didn't choose so much
as let the motion of time take her.

Not for herself, but for her children
not yet conceived
who were already pulling her forward
by the handles of her valise
a suitcase full of dirt and longing.

There wasn't enough for the trip.
They had to borrow more
she would never be able to repay
would never see them again
though she didn't know that yet
nor could she conceive of how
long the line of suffering
one war nearly over and several more
yet to come, reverberations into a present
so shadowy she could only sigh and breathe

because here she was, sitting
on her damp satchel
trying to remember her own name
and stuttering for the first time
in a new language
that felt heavier than her bag.

Azure

Mamaloshen

She woke in a strange place
    they called it home, *heym*
        speak English
        forget your mother tongue.

Green paint chipped off
    tenement walls
        barley and mould.

On the cobblestones below
    an argument rose
        winding into the apartment
        wrapping around her thin neck
            settling as an ache behind her eyes.

Her skin was peeling too
    the edges of her thumb raw
    index finger cracked from humidity
        an unearthly heat
           where was she
           what place, *vas, vau,* was she lost?

She had left willingly
    the preparation seemed endless
        the moment when she stepped
        onto the ship, instantaneous

history dissipating
    places and faces
        she would never see again, her eyesight
        already beginning to fail.

She was young still
        but gravity
                pulls everything down.

Was it home, back there
        if everyone who once formed
                that nucleus was gone?

She stirred the tea, closing her eyes
        directing energy into the samovar
                she had lugged 8,641 kilometres
                        the certainty of facts
                                her father's heavy hand against hers

                it wasn't what she took that weighed her down
                        it was what she left
                                the groove between her mother's brow
                                        the roar of villagers coming.

It was a lifetime ago.
        The tea settled, and she drank slowly
                thick liquid warmed her throat
                        smoke, malt, salt on a smooth cheek

        the lodgers would be home soon
                she had to work.

A question blew in the broken window
        of the brownstone
                not from a physical distance
                        the querent was present
                                layered like clothing
                                on a sweltering body, Baltic wool

whispering from the future
small tea leaves formed lines
approaching the handle.
a pattern she could read:

You will never return
you are not alone; I will speak for you
you are already home.

Space Between Worlds

In the space between worlds, slippage
soft air against her neck
night on her fingers

everywhere ached in colour blocks
a sunrise palette, familiar and not
the same sun, the same rotating planet

bird songs filled her morning
layered as stripes, as sound fields
the gentle yellow chirrup of an Eastern Phoebe
foregrounded by Blue Jay caw
the mad staccato of the Northern Cardinal
she was surprised how many songs
a busy city carried

they were not the birds she knew
running in the woods
behind her village
horse and cart, Sunday market
Sabbath school, people who knew
the day of her birth, her trajectory
waiting on a letter, gathering in secret.

Gadwall, Northern Pintail
Red-crested Pochard gliding
through waterlilies

names her grandfather had taught her
another life, she reached for his hand
found her own small bones
still growing

short chip notes form a spectrogram
sheet music, left to right, high notes to low

this is where the story begins
with sound
shadows and light
the rest is inferred.

There are scents carried
in the skin, images that need no album

longing grows into a song
the one she grew up with
mother-tongue

signature of an endemic species
a long way from home
that other place
which wouldn't wash out in the light

every sound is episodic, hue
brightness, saturation
oscillating, calling out

she leaned into it
tasting the newness, reaching back
and forward simultaneously
pause outside of time.

Between the Ocean and the Stone

Between the ocean and the stone
there is breath
      slow inhale
            slower exhale

every moment
the unwounded body
      uncurls
            a seamless space
                  remains secretly open.

Divination

She learned to hide her gift
in the folds of her skin
         subdermal pockets.

Once, at the dinner table
she predicted the future
swirling smoky tea remains
         an emerging pattern.

A trick passed through the maternal
line: her mother's mother's mother
whispering the future from kitchen counters
         few men ventured.

The cup fell from the table
         leaves scattered onto rotting floorboards

her thoughts scattered too, shame
reddening her cheeks
         limb of the body of the divine.

Liquid seeped onto the dirt
below the house
a secret never to be found
mingled with her blood
         the price of indiscretion.

Her body was changing, shifting
         she swallowed the evidence.

Desire and knowledge are dangerous
        especially for girls.

Know how to raise up
        there were reparations to be made.

She was small, so very small
curled in the old armchair
she would soon leave behind
yet no amount of shrinking
could stop her seeing
        what she saw.

Manhattan, Assembly District 8

Council District 8 includes Manhattan, El Barrio, parts of the Bronx, Central Park and Randall's Island.

Randall's Island once held a poorhouse and burial ground, a home for juvenile delinquents, another for civil war veterans, and an insane asylum. The House of Refuge was not a refuge. Poor Irish boys were hung by their thumbs by the mostly drunken officers who ran the place.

In the Bronx of 1910 it was not yet the roaring twenties. Nothing was roaring for them except sewing machines.

She found her way to the Shirtwaist Factory via one of the lodgers, who heard from a friend that they were hiring. No English necessary. English was, in fact, undesirable – a potential route to unionisation, strictly forbidden.

She had begun to learn, her ability to understand outstripped her ability to speak, but it was easy to pretend she knew nothing.

Azure

Białowieża Forest
primeval foliage
    weaving through her dreams

no words for the smell of
    moss on a fallen trunk

light against her cheek
    a space only in childhood
      not a place
        or even a time anymore
        lost in a humectant bubble

nothing is more permanent
    than something lost

the Azure Tit she once found
    its tiny white belly
      still warm
      soft blue of broken wings
they don't make blue like that anymore

the ghosts of bison and elk
    hovered in memory
      like the emperor oak
        damp bark beneath her feet as she
        hid from the men

        boots flattening everything living

here there is no bark
      no forest crunch
            only concrete

the high pitched dee dee dee
      of the Tit's song
            replaced by tram clank and rumble
      children yelling
            a continuous murmur
    with the urgent motion
            of present tense
      like a small bird
            its lifeless body still warm
                  drawing her back.

A Devout Child

She wasn't always afraid of sunlight.

There was a time in the first month
sitting on Orchard Beach
looking up at pink clouds in motion
with something one might call gratitude.

It was Sunday in the new world
a new job tomorrow: seamstress.

Her mouth strained at the word
wrapping around the English
she was slowly learning
though it still hurt
pressed at the edges of her tongue
forcing a focus
that caused her head to ache.
A job.
She would be safe now.

Her foot slid back and forth in sand
waves came in, went out
time expanded and space contracted.

The great body of water stretched
to a horizon she knew
would continue fading
from green to blue to grey
all the way to the Russian Empire
Atlantic Ocean to Baltic Sea.

She closed her eyes
let the warmth
move into her chest.

She recognised the moment
imagined since she was a child
praying quietly
at the back of the Great Synagogue

large white colonnades
wooden bench worn smooth
fingers pressed together
lips moving silently
in another language
an easier one.

It wasn't so far away.
Maybe in a different universe
this body of hers
still occupied that bright space.

Cairn

When the light   was right
        filtered   through
   home-made curtains
       in her tiny   Bronx kitchen
  she sometimes   was able
       to conjure   sounds
   the great reed warbler   *peep peep*

or see a pygmy owl
       silently   swooping
along   the Neman river
  she walked   with a cousin
  at night   long ago
     more dream now   than memory

they knelt   into snowfall
  piling a mound
      flat   granite stones
   large on   the bottom
    smaller on top

to find their way
back home
    in time for dinner

the owl's shadow
followed them
to the fire   the stew
the sweet burn   of her fingers
when gloves   came off

nowadays   we know
not to   build cairns

rocks   belong to wildlife
      shelter   nesting space

holding her breath   counting
five   four   three   two   one
      in the old language   of course
there was   no magic in English

she was able to   recreate the cold
hear the sweet   warble of the Tit
feel the   brush of wings
        on her   stooped back
aching   from too many hours
in the   sweatshop

but no matter the language
            she couldn't   find the stones
            to guide   her home.

Land of the Immigrant

There is always breakage
it's not always visible, inside a small
unassuming house
beneath a common roof
a place you've almost certainly
never heard of (*it barely exists*).

She folded her story into fabric
grated it into potato latkes
spoke softly, a girlish voice in a language
you almost certainly wouldn't recognise
*(though it does exist, seeping in
through the cracks in time).*

Does this story need to be told?

She's reading it again for the third time
crying into cracked eggs
rocking slightly with fear and love
her small body leaning against the stovetop.

Should we let her sleep
leave the photos where they are
a box in the cupboard, fading?
Who gets to decide?

The guidebook is in Yiddish
covered in food stains, ragged edges
thumbed and shared between dreamers
who want nothing more
(neither record nor reckoning)

than to walk down the street
ghostly and silent
until it's safe enough
through a conduit of a blood
for a great-grandchild, older
than the tiny forgotten woman
shivering besides the flame
to look right into those dark hidden
spaces and sing.

Fish Smoker

Third Avenue EL

Iron wheels on metal track. Steep steps,
ragged breath, platform.

The train shakes her apartment twice a day
but this is the first time she takes it.

People in the street below are small, working.
She thinks of her village back home.

Her father sings softly, writing letters
to the Immigrant Aid Society
asking for help.

Everything happens slowly
until she suddenly shifts.

Now she is already here
high above the city
waiting for a train to go collect a letter.

From this angle the city is just
variations in tone: concrete
lines of track playing against shadows.

Her parents might be just past the horizon point
in a little house, doing the things they'd always done
tending to herbs, cooking, washing.

She knew that war was coming
but they would surely be safe.

The letter would reassure her
waiting at the downtown
post office with news

while the train went shush clack
against along the rails
her view obscured through smoked glass.

Maybe tomorrow
she would open her apartment door
with the broken bell and in they would come
tired but flushed from travel, carrying tattered suitcases.

They would sit in her kitchen and eat soup.
Her mother, bless her, would complain that it was bland.

In the meantime, she stepped
quickly over the gap between the train
and the platform into the lower east side
with all of its noise and promise
fingers crossed against the inevitable.

Like light in a dream

How many letters did she send
before one was finally answered

the address was wrong
handed to her by a neighbour
who recognised the name

a thin card with torn edges
already old, her mother's shaky
Yiddish, smudged

long life to you my Rivka
we pray every day to hear
how you are getting on
in your new life
her charmed life

bodies in Odessa were thrown
by police into the Black Sea
or buried in the fields

this is what she heard
around the sewing machines
gossip or news
she would never know

she stroked the worn card
felt the miles it had travelled
a migrant like her
uncertain of its end point

she would write back immediately
another letter, and another
they would not have
to pray for a letter
from their lost daughter

the needle on her Singer
moved up and down
while she pushed the fabric through
her back curved over
all day long the machines chanted
cash cash cash cash
save save save save.

Peddlers

Colour equalled sound
      each knock on the door
      had a pattern.

Two two one two
      pins, combs, soaps and cloth
      red blue yellow brown.

She felt the vibrations in her
      body, a slight jump
      a quiver in her stomach.

A voice in Yiddish
      Goods, *skhoyres*
      What's in the bag?

There were other noises
      a horn for fish
      wa wah wee
      Ya-aleh ve-yavo
      not today, thanks.

Smoked lox was a luxury
      brought back on occasion
      barrel-ends, strong smelling
      good for the baby he said
      in the early days.

A bell for knife sharpeners
>ringing everyone out of stupor
>in Belarus red
>the colour of revolution
>she winced, opened the curtain
>no revolution here
>aside from the grinders stone
>rotating squeaky shades of pink.

The milkman said *yike yike*
>a voice coloured creamy white
>light flooding in.

The city was full of them
>carrying baskets, pushing barrows
>hollering in every language.

When she was a child
>she excelled at math
>numbers moved around her head
>in visual patterns
>each with its own colour.

She knew about money
>what to spend, when to argue.

Who would bother
>with department stores
>where overdressed women
>looked you up and down
>lipstick curling downwards
>when everything came to the door.

Pickled Herring Pushcart

What if I walked backwards
into the tableau and just
sat with the fish smoker.

Yes, I know he has a name
it was not the one he used.

A thin young man, somewhat short
eyes already showing signs of anger
but still hopeful, taking care
over his appearance
wavy hair showing beneath
a wool newsboy cap.

Turning the handle with sincerity
in some crack between our worlds
where we could speak freely

a modern woman, a handsome Jew
the resemblance between them
oblivious to time.

He might take my hands
in his, rough against the
softness of my own
an ease he earned for me
with ice and toil.

Whisper everything
so I might understand
contrition and trauma
in equal measure.

Leaning against the relative
safety of his pushcart
our lives frozen into photographs
black and white with faded edges
but still vital
pulsing like Hester Street
crowded even in the early hours.

Diddikai

Her first lodging was with Italian migrants
a Bronx walk-up smelling of sausage.
Fingers throbbed in the unheated room
as she scrubbed the floor
hiding the bottles
accumulating illegally in the hall
dodging dangerous boys with ragged breath
swearing she would never
let a man like that touch her
in this ugly new world.

Then she met the fish smoker.
He was more charming than any man she'd met
his smile wide as the Black Sea.
He smelled of home
whispering the mother-tongue in her ear.

She had learned to read tea leaves
from her mother's mother
her future in tannin dreams, grandchildren
in southern lands
with names she didn't yet know.

When he showed up for the second time
dancing for her with light feet
that seemed to hover above icy cobblestones
she ignored the warning
spelled by her tea, breath condensed with longing
in the ancient kitchen, with the cracked linoleum
and broken kettle that burnt her small hands

twice a day
and gave in without hesitation.

Every Poem is a Lie

There is no dissembling here, no truth to be verified
in a court of what did and didn't take place.

There is only desire. This is where it begins.
It may be that all there is to know has already been

uncovered and there is only conjecture from here on in
so why not go straight to where it hurts.

Where it hurts is the point of entry, a wormhole.
There is no such thing as time. We talk of passing,

cause and effect, tag something as a beginning, arbitrarily.
We cannot live unbounded and so.

One: Arrival, disembarking a crowded ship, dirty
hungry, not just for food. Into a new life, two people

unknown to one another, linked by proximity, nostalgia
or anguish. Dark heads with different dreams.

Two: they both entered the job market within a week. The census
said fish smoker. For her, *nothing*, though we know

she was a seamstress, working without formalities, a tiny job
in a big space. It always comes down to profits.

He was an educated man, brother, dancer, linguist, gaucho
a woman's man masquerading as a man's man

weighed down by herrings, lox, whitefish, you'd be surprised
at what needs to be smoked. It was hard work, honest.

That's what they called it. It paid the rent, just. Hers was a world
where shirts mattered. Labour was needed, her hands

small enough. No one wrote it down. Nowadays they say
undocumented. Words break down under scrutiny.

Three: the beginning of something else. Let's call them hobbies,
or perhaps that's too glib. Ancillary activities.

For him, a nightly tipple, bootleg whisky, a flutter, extra cash.
For her the reading of tea leaves.

These are voices that might endure, under the right kind
of pressure, like diamonds. What if she pays some of the bills

from her readings, a small group of regulars lining up
to learn the future. It might be a lie, magic, or something

entirely different, born of everything that she left
soft crooning, *sleep little bird: Shlof mayn feygele.*

The story will not end here.
Though time is illusory, we have to begin. She opens

the window of her tiny apartment and light fills the kitchen.

Bear of a Man

He was studying to become a Rabbi
until he lost his faith.

He never spoke of it
once he let go
he never got it back.

Faith is a fickle beast
its absence thick and dark as a bear.
He could not unsee the void.

He spoke eleven languages.
One must have been English
from there we have
Spanish — the brothers migrated first
to Argentina where they learned
to drink like cowboys — his undoing
but that was later. Hebrew,
Yiddish (*mother tongue*)
Polish, Russian (*borders were always
changing — it was best to be prepared*).

What the others were is conjecture.
He told stories of the old country
in the Shtetl, acting the role of the men
and women of the neighbourhood
eyes rolling, hands flailing
everyone doubled over with laughter.

Though he was big, he was graceful
dancing on china plates without
so much as a chip.

Later he broke tables
overturning the cards when he lost.
Later he broke bones
but only when drunk
and only occasionally.

La Grippe

Let's say you wake up one morning covered in a cold sweat. Your pyjamas are so wet you wonder if you've had an accident.

You cannot get out of bed although you are not paid for days you don't go to work and you need the money to feed your family – that's one wife and four children, not all of whom are born as yet, but the pressure of their need is mingling with your fever and you feel it along the length of your spine like a line of fire. It's a pressure that will never let up, except when you've got enough of the drink in you to dull the ache and of course on the day your body finally lets go, prematurely, liver first.

People call it the Bolshevik disease, accused your people of bringing it into the country in battered suitcases eleven years prior, then waiting for the right moment to unleash those unholy germs on an otherwise pristine nation. Not true, of course, though there is no way you can deny it, your once powerful voice breaks against the limits of a language no longer new. You will not be eloquent again.

On arrival, the authorities checked everyone thoroughly for fevers, tuberculosis, typhus, cholera, leprosy. Sick people were marked with an X. If you were sick you went to hospital three. Isolation ward. Detention. You couldn't leave until you were healthy. It was not a desired outcome.

You left Ellis promptly. No incriminating X stained your jacket. The line of people you were in didn't stop moving. The only thing that stopped was the watch you carried, held fast in your pocket, a silver antique your father had given you when you turned thirteen. It could never could be made to start again. That was the smallest price you had to pay for leaving.

She brings you soup through the illness. Everyday, feeds it to you off a small teaspoon, thick and hot, burning your parched throat on the way down. She has a gentle touch. Walks without noise, her dark eyes soft with sympathy. Nor does she get sick — at least not her body. The cold compress on your head. The endless bowls. She is there whenever you open your eyes and you vow that when you get better you will take more care of her, this silent bird who flew only once, this fragile beauty dripping borscht between your lips.

And when you got better? Ach, fish smoker, you cannot change the past. It wends its way through the funhouse of time in antigenic drift and shift, viral particles infecting the future.

Potatoes

Some days it was only barley broth. Some days
a few bits of squashed herring
brought home from the bottom
of the barrel, his legs purple
from standing in ice water all day.

*She arrived at the apartment before him, her hands
shaking as she cut up what food she could find,
cabbage mostly, purchased cheap from
the vegetable peddler, fit only for stewing.*

If there was bread, it was so hard
she needed a hammer to break it.

*Dizzy, hair spilling from her combs
she would tuck it behind the ears
ignoring the migraine that began in the morning
at the sewing machine, all day at the machine
with no breaks, fingers throbbing.*

It was not the life she'd dreamt of, curled
under a thin blanket during the Russian winter.
The streets here were not paved with gold, after all.

*Tomorrow there might be windows that opened
hot running water, a proper flushing toilet,
potatoes. These were her new dreams.*

She tried, without success, to sweep away
the grime that encrusted the floor
to wash the smells of rotting cabbage
and smoked fish from her clothing.

The scent followed her to work, where her
sewing machine kept going until the bell rang
and she never drank water because the door
to the toilet was broken and the toilet was so dirty
she feared becoming ill by using it.

She bent over, her young back hunched as she
leaned into the machine trying to forget the pain
that followed her like a faithful dog
the rest of her life, and she got used to it.

She never told him about the way her body
continuously hurt, carried her pain silently
into the shared space
no one wanted to call home.

Sugar

She knew nothing about the pancreas
she didn't even know she had one.

Insulin was a word only scientists knew
she was not a scientist, but she was bright

her hand went up first at school before she left
she could calculate sums like a boy

diligently working at her books, dark hair piled
on top of her head, biting her lip in concentration.

These details had been lost somewhere
in the Baltic sea. In their place, a fissure.

Even at twenty her body was breaking down
vision going, kidneys straining, blood sugar rising.

She knew something was wrong, but what could she do
there was work to be done.

Her thirst knew no bounds, though there was precious
little change for sweets sometimes

the girls would pass around a Luden's cough
drop – lemon menthol. If you were caught sneezing

or clearing the throat, dismissal.
No food on the table, no wine to warm him up

no mercy. He called her crazy. She struggled to think clearly.
her hands were always shaking, even at the sewing machine

it took all her energy to focus. Nine hours, ten, tack
tack, needle against fabric. The effort drained her.

In another lifetime she would get treatment
but she didn't have one.

Ephemeral Washington Square

Sometimes something shifted.

Maybe it was the way
    light glinted off asphalt at 8am
        when she disembarked from the streetcar

        into a hustle of steam, clop and squeak of horse drawn carts
            clank, putter, whistle into the park, past the marble arch
    rising like an invitation, engraved, an exhortation
        the round fountain radiating outward
            symmetros
                children in bathers yelling
                  electric green grass
            the shuffle of feet going somewhere

        she was going somewhere

    absorbing the energy of so many bodies
        a million dreams, a thousand daytime stories
            glossolalia *he said and then she said*
            excuse me, no excuse me, sorry!

        City air, soft against her cheeks
        secondhand hat pulled low over escaping curls
    vendors in carts and umbrellas
        ice cold lemonade 5c a glass, sizzling frankfurters
            sweet California apples 6c
    her heels clacking against cobblestones
        cross Greene Street to Washington Square East.

This was a story she was part of
    unfolding like a book in brown brick
    a corner building, triangular

  the particular echoing silence
    of a crowded stairwell
        the lift broken again

            where she walked right up to the ninth floor
                past fabric bins overflowing with scraps
                                and cutters
        tables, hanging fabrics surrounding
            and punched a mechanical clock like a hundred
                                other
        girls each from somewhere not here and squeezed
        into her dark spot for another factory day.

Beyond the Pale

A Careless Cigarette

March 25th, 1911.
She cannot find the energy
to lift the curtain.

The lamp light flickers
it's not yet morning and if she doesn't
get up she will lose her job.

The room is unheated, a claw-foot bathtub
in the kitchen. She bathes quickly
using water from the stove.

Above her, faded wallpaper peels
from the corner, steam condenses.

He has already left.
Morning is a silent affair.
There are no children yet but they are
coming, coming, coming
though it all hangs in the balance
in this moment
where she has yet to decide.

She tries to eat but she is dizzy
work to home, home to kitchen
kitchen to bed, a simple equation
that doesn't add up on this day.

They need the money
but her head wavers like fever
Shtetl dreams
a rooster forever crowing
the neighbour's dog
the smell of black tea
which she has over-brewed
this morning of all mornings
black leaves congealing
into a warning.

She drops the cup, tea spilling onto the floor
crawls back into bed, her small body
heavier than it will ever be again
weighed down with prescience.

She shivers and sleeps through the day
her mind plays tricks.

In her dream she sews shirts
long rows of machines
fill the top floor
of the Triangle Shirtwaist Factory
where they lock the exits
so the girls won't take a break
or leave without first emptying
their pockets and handbags
for the groping foreman.

She is not the only one
who speaks little English
her back hunched over
flammable white cotton.

The teacup remains broken on the floor
where the fish smoker will find it, returning home
with the news that the factory
has burned down.

One hundred and forty six fellow workers
burnt and asphyxiated
pushing against doors
that would not open
broken on the concrete below
where they jumped, living torches
inside the cordon.

She wakes to find out
that she has lost her job
but not her life.

He will bend that day with gratitude
later forgotten
clean up the spilled tea
and broken china.

However he arranges the pieces
he cannot repair the cup
or the cracks that have opened
beneath her skin.

The Consequence of Silence

A distant object can appear to travel faster
than the speed of light
across the line of sight, across a body of time.

> There were voices from her china cup
> a backdrop of peeling paint
> aluminium saucepans, smells
> familiar as a Grodno kitchen
> the Neman River winding
> Belarus to Lithuania.

Unstitch the moment connecting her to me
without the need for modern inventions
no telephone, internet, rocket ship
with warp bubble stretching the fabric
of spacetime in a wave. It is already now.

> She climbed the walk-up step after step
> *child after child,* she was pregnant again
> though I'm the only one who knows
> at this early stage, leaning into the space
> of our shared DNA, that she will lose this one
> bleeding alone in the bathroom
> learning, not for the first time, *to keep quiet.*

Her tears wet my face
trauma and silence bind us.

> English is brutal, its edges sharp
> outlined in spittle.

She watches the door open, sees him turn
knows he's left everything behind for this grind
the long walk, *every damned day*
the headaches, the constant noise.

       Unable to let go, he's kept at it
       his arms strengthened
       by all the wooden barrels he lifts.
       and drunk with loss
       he strikes.

Beyond the Pale

When light came   through the broken
        window   splintering
                as diamonds against linoleum
        she felt it

it was morning   in the new world.
  Yiddish   voices
    whispered by neighbours through
        thin walls

a soothing sound   filtered
            into her bedroom   cold wind

it wasn't   Russian-winter   cold
        but   the heater   didn't work
                her bed   was empty

he was asleep   couch again
        third night   in a row
            she picked the bottle   off the floor
    empty cup   on its side

the baby crying
        wouldn't   wake him
unless she let it   go
    more than   a minute
        if that   happened

she would find out fast
there is no such   thing
      as shelter

she lifted   the baby
      from his   wooden cradle

her son's hair was   fine   soft
   so blond
   it was   almost white
      which made   no sense
         as both of them   were dark as Sephardi

her lips   against the child's head
            the scent of   milk   and lotion
sent warmth   across her   collar bone

she had never   been able   to hold onto anger
         it flowed out   wetting her shirt
               her sorrow   a whispered song
                     in the old tongue
            moving through   veins of time

the man   on the sofa
      a person she   once relied on
               no more than a shadow
                     while   enriched
               by her own   *forgiveness*
      she was
               momentarily   untouchable.

Silence and Monkeys

She was not musical

kept quiet
to avoid setting off
        the bear inside him

he hated dirty floors.

If she kept the house clean
if she didn't blink too hard
if she didn't hum
        beneath her breath

she would make it
        to tomorrow

though there was always an urge
        to let go and scream

break every chipped dish
the monkey box chattering
and whining
        across the surface of her skull

let me out let me out

when she was trying
        so hard to be still.

Invisible Strokes

Running along
the collar bones
like a necklace
worn without pride
a coloured rash

a string of decisions
that might not
have been made
had she taken
more time

time was what she didn't have
the clock on the wall ticked
reminding her what
had happened already
and what was yet to come

she needed no reminders
memories were written
into her skin
edged in tiny circles of
blue, red, yellow

hand against the bruise
pressing into the mark
meted out in careful parcels
a retribution
she would never understand.

Love Wounds

It was the fourth labour
if you don't count the losses

she didn't count
they were part of what she carried
pain written into her hips
as she bore down

a doctor whose name was already lost
told her she might not survive another
but here she was, the weight,
a daughter, tearing her open
a wound of love.

The boys would leave her
had already begun the dismantling
laughing cruelly in the hallway
dropping towels like tears
shoving their way into the future

she would not take her family for granted
counting lost cousins
missing aunts
trails left by feet
dragged in the dirt
a generation disappeared

in the new world everything happened
in present tense

the boys took what they needed
slipped out without a backwards glance

her precious daughter
dark hair crowning
would not be so careless.

Pomegranates

There were two thousand acres
in the carpet of her mind
or one yard of cracked linoleum
and a chipped kitchen sink
in which she bathed the baby

on the wall a still life of fruit
dispersed on a table
an appearance of abundance
a not quite satiating
gift from her mother

with a tiny note and nothing more
Remember?

arriving in a torn package
after she started sewing
before she met him
before *la grippe*
before the fire, before children
a lifetime
passing in blood red strokes
her childhood acrylics

she tried to track time with her pinky
tracing bold black outlines

the air was fruity in the summer
      her boy's hair no longer blond
            there were no pomegranates
                in the city
      only a broken vase
the memory of a basket

purple paint, orange flowers
arils large and bright
almost, but not quite, real.

Words are Bullets

He called her cunt.

The children heard the word
past spoons clanking
their singing and dancing
      dinner routine.

The boarder looked up
from a scrappy meal
his neck
      took the shock

      a fast twist
halted by the thud
of a whiskey glass
the crack of the C, the nasal N
      the plosive T.

It hit her like a bullet
left a hole
      visibly smoking.

She said nothing didn't
      even breathe in.

Her twelve-year-old daughter's
already exquisite voice
stopping abruptly mid-song.

She thought to herself
sticks and stones
but her arms were the sticks
      her bones the stones.

Tar Beach (Kelly Street)

The empty roof provided an illusion of privacy
tar softened against summer heat

skin warmed, water tank, birds-eye view
the city skyline she dreamt as a child, *paradise*

some days it was, shoulders bare, towel beneath
the roar of the elevator train like waves against sand

other days, she saw nothing but the past, the acrid smell
made her head ache, her arms heavy with too much knowledge

she stood near the edge, eyes red against the fumes
imagining what it would feel like to go over

the streets below were full of busy people
with destinations. Her destination could end at this point

she might land without a sound, her body
broken against the pavement, the city, the not so new world.

The Body is an Instrument

Nickel Empire

When the subway opened, the elevated station
    became a portal
        it wasn't *Melovyye Karyery,*
            white chalky shores, green-blue water
                that became greener and bluer in memory
                    cerulean, cobalt stannate, endless skyscape
                        her mother's arms out wide spinning

no, here was pure sound, the children's pockets
    jangling with nickels home-made swimmers
        a basket full of food walking across the promenade
            the boardwalk, the sound of the Atlantic Ocean
                lapping indifferent to the growing crowds, hotdogs
                    red hots, ice cream dripping down the arm, *sprinkles*

mama! shrieking gulls, 5c Skeeball
    prizes hanging, *I want a stuffed monkey!*
        little Eva singing the whole length of the boardwalk
        right into the ocean

sea salt and sarsaparilla on Surf Avenue
    even the fish smoker was smiling, sober, corny jokes
        pirouetting passed *The Dreamland Circus* sideshow
            gentle temporary grace
                her eldest, not yet fitted with a beige army uniform
                swore he would play spoons
                    for Lionel the Dog-Faced Boy

they could not afford the rides
but the sand was free, the sunshine cost nothing
the day's peace which would not last
beyond the train ride home
priceless.

Another War

Six newsboys crowded together on the pavement
       below her kitchen

child bodies holding a weight of paper, ragged shorts, bad shoes
she leaned against the old side table, smooth wood
eyes squinting
       Extra extray! Live story!
       German troops invade Poland.
       Nazis bomb Warsaw.
       Read all about it!

the radio on static

in the years since she went alone
       into the wide world
              she'd become bilingual
       even her dreams were in English

       yet there were no words in any language, old or new
       to express what she felt.

       Her boys dressed in crisp tan
       sleeves rolled, hair slicked neatly beneath a garrison cap.

       Her daughter's victory rolls
       black hair, escaping
       like hers always did
       red lips for Uncle Sam
               Born on the 4th of July
               Extra Extray!

The wide world was up in smoke
    her body buckled against newsprint

        she'd waited for a letter, sent what money she could spare
            the last reply *Marry rich,*
            New York is full of millionaires, nu?

        She wrote back
            I've married for love – the American way.

        She pushed the buttons on the radio
        twisted the dial, eventually got a song.

Big voices in small bodies
    the clomp of horses and carriages
    Extra extray!
    So much news and no answers.

        She'd tried to save but he found her tin
            drank the money
                extray!

her fingers picked up the black ink
on yesterday's paper, old news

time was closing in
    the wide world
        had begun to shrink.

Operation Barbarossa

A friend of a friend who might have been a cousin
    stopped her in the street
        They have taken the villagers.

she looked at him blankly
    Who has taken? What villagers?

his eyes were the colour of Dresden china
    milky blue, too big for his face
        he waved his hand like a warning
           but what could she do?

He spoke quickly, breath ragged
    she waited for him to calm, and then he said *Grodno*
        her home, her parents, yellow star, *Wehrmacht*
           the unified forces of the Third Reich.
        one oppressor to another
           she looked up at the empty sky.

Some went to camps
    others were taken to the a neighbouring village
        and shot, some went into the forest (her forest)
        and didn't come out again.
        The city began to recede behind them.

How? Who told you?
    Newspapers say they have
        cleansed the city of Jews.

Have you had letters?

I sent money and letters but the last two came back.

He rocked on his feet, legs impossibly thin, and shrugged

No, nothing. I have a sister. I expect her to arrive

any day.

He played with a loose piece of skin

on his thumb

a small vein pulsed on his head.

Memorial Fountain (Bryant Park)

On the ghost train, the names have faded
warm water splashes gently, memorial fountain
pennies on the bottom, Lincoln one side
wheat sheaf the other
she counts them for luck

every breath is an act of violence
colonising other people's stories
pieced together with saliva and string
charged with the awkward power of the living

she opens a paper, eyes blurring, deciphers
Yiddish letters, trying not to show
the pain while she reads

her mother pushed back her hair
the day she left
a barely exhaled puff into the air
travelling on that endless railway car across time
slowly burning, dawn breaking behind a shadow

she traces the words with her hands
an axiom

her own children were growing too quickly
babies to children, children to adult
in stark black and white
continuing to ask a question, unanswered

will you be there at the end of this trip
when I reach the destination
to which I am going, like a good boy
a good girl.

News from the Old World

The city had begun
> to invade her dreams

air tasted of black pepper
> sunlight burnt her skin

in the morning
she did not recognise
the spaces she had inhabited at night
singing a song
> never sung before
> high pitched
> against the roar of the streets

falling again and again
> the shock of slippage
> the world moving
> > suddenly, unaccountably

in the beginning there were letters
> carefully written script
> in the old language
> > tissue paper, held together by tears

gedenk mikh
remember me
> an old-fashioned hand

there was no space in the apartment
    but she said *come please*
        there is a home here for you
        Mame, bitte kumen

she sent money, little but regular
    letter after letter
    no one came
        other than a stream of unknown immigrants
        filling the building, Yiddish, Italian, Irish
        but mostly Yiddish

she could close her eyes and imagine
    she was in the Shtetl still
    talking to the old man across the road
        pants tied with string
        her own children shaking their heads
        speak English, Ma

the words had a logic, like time
    a progression which could be
        counted on the fingers
        flipped through on a paper calendar
        a boy yelling out the news

war after war after war
    remember me, gedenk mikh
    she did not have enough fingers
    to count the dead.

The frailty of parchment

The letters lay dormant
      diaphanous, candlelight, wooden table
            patch of moonlight formed a shaft

she was dreaming of an ocean
      light rays on water, rising warmth
            lost summer

in the darkness there was sun
      somewhere, fingers warming fountain pen
            someone looking back at her ghostly

the world was so big
      a sequence of events in parchment
            scribbled notes, shaky last words ink stained, fading

she had nothing else to work with
      only this sense of knowing, her body temporarily safe
            her mind caught in a whirlwind

beyond the sea she travelled, one thousand years ago
      one million light years, arbitrary markers
            lifetimes, clocks in orbit

she inhaled sharply, picking up a blank sheet from the small pile
      that particular texture, crisp against her fingers
            so many voices crowded in, what would she say

who would she address,
        shoemaker, shoeshiner, Schumacher
                her father's hands were long and thin, curling and uncurling

Are you safe? Are you happy?
        she lifted her leaking pen, ink settled into the lines of a finger
                how would she find them again

to weave the story *forgive me*
        Jacob's ladder, to heal the pain
            heat rose in her cheeks

                    seventy rungs
                      like the end of days.

Spoons

In spite of the blackouts
the slips she couldn't contain

in long stretches of silence
she had given birth to children

who knew how to entertain
her eldest reached into the

kitchen drawer one day
pulled out an idiophone

in the form of a spoon
when he picked them up

he did not think soup
stew, porridge, the way she did

he heard music
notes swirling in the air

his body moving in time
shoulders jerking, spoons colliding

the body is an instrument
metal on metal on flesh

in the vibration of that sound
flatware became symphony

the air alive, laughter
and clacks, light flashing

through the darkness, a song of joy
she recognised.

Eva Stormgirl

Eva was born into a storm
rain blew into the curtains
as she screamed for the first
but not the last time

her eyes glowed lavender
before settling to hazel green

her need in that moment was great
as it is for all newborns

too quickly other needs
outflanked hers

she learned to read the room
her mother's tears, the ink
of her education

her father needed
to be watched carefully

when the house
was full of drinking
card-playing men
dangerous, bloodshot, aroused
she taught herself to shrink
faded her outline
slipped in and out of view
like a ghost

it was a skill she would return to
long after the shrapnel
of her father's prodigious anger
created scars that wouldn't heal
for generations, silver marks
on the highway of Eva's legacy
where the sublimated burst forth
in streams of broken light
reflecting all her father had lost
and all she would
have to sing back into being.

Goodie Basket

Nothing   could contain
        the unearthly beauty
                of Eva's voice   powerful enough

to break glass   to time-travel
        to unfurl the trauma   of her DNA
                to heal beyond the span of a life

the gift she was born with
        her brothers   taught her
                to use it   well

sustaining notes above one hundred
        decibels   sound against resonant
                frequency   shattering preconceptions

what she did with it   is another story
        what didn't shatter
                when she   hit the high note

passed   not from her mother
        whose   goodie basket
                included   several generations   of guilt

        a   desire
        to mother the   world

        the whole   lost neighbourhood
        held   in those skinny arms

strangers   unleashing all manners
        of pain   sorrow   loss   she
            sopped up   her body a sponge

the voice   was his
        a birdsong   he recognised
            felt the loss of   mourned

long after   the whisky buzz faded
        and his body   escaped
            the prison   of lost dreams.

Single Vernacular

His daughter could not remember
        the man he was before bootleg whiskey

prohibition and poverty did not
        cure him of those green bottles

his theatrical voice
        slurred to a vernacular

guttural as he slid to the floor
        glass breaking against linoleum

it was his daughter's job
        to pick him up

drag him to bed
        when he passed out

a relief for everyone
        after the fury of intoxication

cards scattered, everything spent
        whatever was broken waiting

to be fixed or discarded
        shrapnel of a thwarted intellect

swept into the bin, tidied
        into the silence of history.

Tikkun Olam

Low Chroma (Coney Island, 1946)

Eyelids down, body on damp rock
there is no day or night, only rotation
this close
ultraviolet might be visible
as to a hummingbird
fired in a harlequin kiln
against hillside moss

cold wax scratches out a lexicon
in the gap between desire and memory
paying homage to absence
capturing only what is present

from here there is no longing
only breath
steady against filtered light
forest as body
line and form
carbon dioxide and oxygen
each breath a promise

outside this space
there is so much noise it is impossible
to pick out shards of meaning
emerge unscathed from the undergrowth
re-engage with the river

sound has gravity, travelling
through solid rock as wind, thunder, argument
breaking through the silence
punching in

if humans could photosynthesise
taking nutrients from sun would we
change, become greener, not just our skin

voices softening to a whisper
linking roots beneath the surface
of the earth, finally healing.

Yennevelt

There is no *other world*
> the rough man with a big fist
> whacked the table and swore

this was no ordinary table
> it was Russian oak
> cracked in just the right spot
> smooth underhand, sidewalk strewn
>> a gift from the sky

precious or not it was upended
> regularly during card games he lost
> while she hid in her room
>> the rhythm of a sewing machine
>> drowning out the bluster of men
>> as she practiced disappearing

it wasn't that she didn't like swearing
> or the small tenement she inhabited
>> though the peeling wallpaper
>> and sour smell fell short of her dreams
>> from so many years ago
>>> in a hurried departure
>>> from somewhere that no longer
>>> was anywhere

she was willing to settle in
> let herself go softly
> without a trace on her perfect face
>> this other self, darker, smaller, tougher

than the whimpering mess
she would become
    when the party was over
    and he came to bed

everyone was hungry, of course they were
    her stomach was always grumbling
    you could only go so far
        on barley soup or even the occasional
        whiting from the bottom of the barrel

the gap was never filled
    hunger was not only desire for food

even in this world she was free to dream
    she had the power
        to turn dreaming into a gateway

    not just to another mythical place
    where her art could bloom
        tiny blue flax flowers with green
        dragonflies and bright orange butterflies

a facsimile of home
    closer than she realised
    a parallel universe
        opened via the mother tongue
        charging her bad back and failing eyesight
        disarming her husband's rage
        changing everything.

One Wandering Eye

Amblyopia   her vision
          contracted
   clouds moving   across the surface
pale blue   white   grey
          she let them   drift

muscles moved
          on their own   blinked
          turned her head
          tried to focus   slipped

time is   never
          what you think
she   put her head   down

let it come
          she had   already lost
                    the long skein   the connection
          the thread   back to where
     objects had edges

once   she thought
          to hide   the wandering
                    her face sharp   her mind sharper
          playing   along a thin line

the world   tilted into view
          close   enough to   grab
                    she   found   breath

these days   there is
        only   night
    occasionally   a perfume
        fills the room

    the softness of a   child
        familiar as   memory
            and she knows   grace.

Subject to Dispersal

Small footsteps
up the broken path
      achromatic grey
      like a childhood sky
trailing through a lattice of time

I saw her there
but it was only a dream
      the house lamps flickering
      her hands pressed forward
      as if to say, stop
      don't go further
you will not like what you find

somehow in that space
she was still vital
      tugging at her skirt
      remembering freedom
      as if it were a place
      she might visit in her mind
when daylight dissipates

there were bees on the Primulas
sweet scent like orange lollies

the smell continues
to linger
      even as it dissolves
into a past she can barely access

she was the girl in the picture
moving slowly
       sunlight on her face
another life

yet here she is walking in the sun
the air whistling
       her youthful body in motion
unimpeded

Skeleton Leaf

Age came
> *without preamble*

the thinning of tissues
> *intricately laced veins*

where skin was once smooth

it was still possible to see the girl
> *in her bone structure*

looking outward, sienna ferrotype

eyes bigger
> *than you'd expect*

in such a small face

an expression recognisable
> *longing and resignation*

held in permanent tension

already the body was shrinking
> *the world blurring*

she needed help up the steps
> *stumbled against the door*

burned her hand rendering chicken fat

she leaned against
> *the armchair*

feeling the lightness
> *of her imprint*

from that spot she could conjure
    a lifetime
any moment she thought lost
    ghostly against the window
in shadow
    spaces and places
she'd known and left
    fragile
but no less real.

Kussmaul breathing

The dog is snoring again
she picks up the sound
an early warning radar
pulsing through her body
in the kitchen doorway
as she struggles for oxygen.

Unlike her own harsh rasp
distorting the air around her
the animal makes
gentle, even sounds
the occasional *yip yip*.

He might be chasing
a rabbit in the Elysian Fields
of his mind, such simple pleasures
don't diminish her exaggerated sighs
the growing sense that for her
this is the beginning of the end.

The sensation pervades her fingers
as she stirs the pot, potatoes and carrots
tiny bits of meat for protein
her bones crumbling from within
her mind twisting around the fascia.

The scent is sweet
sharp as she grabs hold
of the chair, holding tight
as if on a moving ship.

So many miles of travel
only to find herself
back in that same dark space.

The dog looks up
his sad eyes mirror
something breaking in her
but not quite yet.

He knows what is coming.

Repairing the World

She was tired, her body slowly
failing against a world that still
needed her

reaching a thin arm outward
towards a future
she was able to read
but didn't understand
long words in tiny print
from the days when her vision
was stronger
so much remained undone

how could she help
repair these wounds
so deep in the body
in the twisted helix of her genome
and deeper, within the world

where would she begin
when her fingers were already
curling in

her husband's Kabbalah
sat on the shelf, its edges yellow
with dust and time

he had long given up
on those studies or any kind
of *mitzvah*

he lived only for oblivion
but would live
another lost decade
she would not find answers there
her hands shook with this last effort

she gathered her final moments
an inward breath pulled from fragile
lungs that once sang Yiddish songs
filling the kitchen
with the old country
laughing
even when there was nothing
to laugh about

whispered magic into lukewarm tea
into the warm autumn air
into her daughter's soft, dark hair
and through that conduit
her daughter's daughter's daughter
passed on a secret sound
that wouldn't be heard
by anyone in the vicinity
above the elevator train
roaring against a setting sun.

Tikkun Olam

The physical universe presses against transparent lids, *hush now,*
ten calibrations of empty space. Her body is failing but there is
something within she can feel but not touch.

Not the shutting organs or nameless pain running along her
spinal cord, not the blurring cooking pot lid clattering on the gas
stove in a mystery language: *kstit kstat hiss hushhh.*

She breathes out sounds: spirit, air, echo, into the tiny apartment.
Past roaches scurrying over linoleum, dust motes, asbestos, peeling
wallpaper. Beyond the cracked windowpane into the city.

Breath condenses, twenty-two letters into the fabric of existence,
dimensions through which a future forms, tentative as skin cracks,
hands dishwasher grey beneath wool gauntlets.

Broken charms on the mantle. In a primordial forest
of lost childhood, she sits on a mossy rock, alive and not,
in this Schrödinger's moment of superposition, where she has

not yet died and I have not yet been born. All her life she has lived
with an illusion of solitude. Even in a roomful of people,
side-by-side sewing machines, the roar of city crowds, drunkards

at the card table, children pulling at apron strings. She believed
her survival nothing more than transgression, like a shark,
eating her way forward. A Boreal owl cries in staccato.

Old growth, decaying wood, an aggregation of all she
thought lost, living and dead, lichens and fungi.
There was so much weight and now she is light, ready to begin.

In the land of the Lenape a space is opened by grief. She hears
a song, not in her native tongue, another, Unami, the familiar
voice of dispossession. Traces the sound along rivers and creeks,

old world and new, the energy of everything that exists.
She never sang like this in life, tamped within her body,
illness, the long arm of memory, a terror she could not shake.

Her eyes glow the shade of forest, open into a timeless,
spaceless landscape, lips wide, letters, numbers, the voice of a girl.
She is alone and surrounded: mutes, sibilants, aspirates, the sacred

text and the world: *hush now*, spectral coordinates along a wavelength
of sound, everywhere green: tea green, sap green, myrtle.
Trees are cathedrals. They have been waiting only for us to arrive.

Human Bandwidth

Travelling east
      sound is a carnival: precarious

            all this industry, the rising damp
              old scent of leaf mould
                  jewels of sap gleaming in the sun

              one eye closed, one sharp gasp
            one more step until the sun goes down
      turning by degrees

she knew the metallic taste
      desiccating skin of this sweet dessert
            the voices of people she lost
              calling, calling

it's not so far
      to that no place of embrace
            arriving from a space already
              deconstructed and recreated
                into another story

              the body is a pattern
            the road it walks upon
      another pattern
    the air that moves
against the skin, pattern

her growing power
    radiates through the pores
       out the skin
          masquerading as warmth
             coalescing into the shape of a body

the forest is my ocean
the ocean is my breath

all the water that runs from me now
is all of the water that ever was.

What Remains

How far back can you go?
You can never go back.

Everything changed – borders
first names, language.
Where are you from?

The answer was arbitrary
and essential.

Mistakes were made on arrival
and stuck. Error became identity
everything shifts
stability is illusion.

Some died en route;
it was a hard trip.
Others were sent back,
their names erased from record.
You will not find them on any census.
No one speaks of them now.

Your mother, her name
no longer part of history
leans over a wooden window frame.

Her eyes have the same softness as yours
that downward slant at the corners
thick dark hair covered by a headscarf
her privacy intact forever
frozen in this space as you walk away.

You tried harder than most to hide
but there are some things
that cannot be hidden.

Magic is a gift not held
solely in fading photographs.

It lingers, like your voice
humming a Yiddish song
winding through the double
helix of your children, filling the air
everywhere.

Notes and Sources

The Pale of Settlement

The Pale of Settlement was a region of the Russian Empire with varying borders that existed from 1791 to 1917 as a means for keeping Jews separated from the rest of the Empire which included modern day Belarus, Lithuania, Moldova, part of the Ukraine, Poland, Latvia, and the Russian Federation. In 1881, Temporary Laws prohibited Jews from settling outside the Pale, and life inside the little towns (Shtetls) of the Pale was poverty-stricken and hard, particularly once the violent riots known as "pogroms" became more prevalent in the early 20th century.

The Black Hundreds

The Black Hundreds were an ultranationalist extremist right-wing monarchist group in early 20th Century Russia, noted for their devotion to the Tsar, who funded their activities, and their brutal anti-semitic pogroms.

Philology

Ashkenazic Jews were among the last Europeans to take family names and only began to do so in the early nineteenth century when compelled by the authorities so they could be taxed.

Guide to the United States for the Jewish Immigrant

The non-italicised text in this poem comes from the *Guide to the United States for the Jewish Immigrant (1916)* by John Foster Carr, Immigrant Publication Society.

Mother of Exiles

"Mother of Exiles" is another name for the Statue of Liberty, and comes from Emma Lazarus' sonnet "The New Colossus", excerpts of which are inscribed on a plaque inside the Statue. The words "sea-washed" are also used in the poem.

Azure

Bialowieza Forest is a large primeval forest located on the border between Poland and Belarus, not far from where Rebecca grew up.

Mamaloschen

Mamaloschen is the Yiddish word for mother-tongue and is often a reference to the Yiddish language itself. Among the Jewish immigrant group of this era, Yiddish was spoken in the home by mothers and grandmothers, while Hebrew was used for religious study and English was the language of commerce.

Third Avenue El

The IRT Third Avenue railway, known as the Third Avenue Elevated, Third Avenue El, or Bronx El, was an elevated railway in Manhattan and the Bronx. It was discontinued in 1973.

La Grippe

The 1918 Spanish Influenza pandemic, sometimes called la grippe, killed between 50 and 100 million people worldwide.

A Careless Cigarette

The Triangle Shirtwaist Factory fire in New York City on March 25, 1911 was the deadliest industrial disaster in the history of the city, and one of the deadliest in US history. The factory was located in the Asch building in Greenwich Village. It was mostly staffed with underpaid female teenage Jewish and Italian immigrants who were forced to work as many as twelve hours a day, seven days a week, with exit doors locked to keep out union organisers. One hundred and forty-six workers died in less than fifteen minutes. Rebecca was an employee at the Triangle Shirtwaist Factory when the fire broke out but for reasons no one knows, she was not at work that day.

Beyond the Pale

Sephardi are Jews from Spain. Also known as Sephardic Jews or Sephardim.

Tar Beach (Kelly Street)

Tar Beach is urban slang for the flat tar surface of a building roof where people sometimes went to sunbathe.

Nickel Empire

When the subway to New York City from the boroughs was completed in the 1920s, the cost of a trip to Coney Island was only five cents (a "nickel"), enabling poor people to travel to the seaside for the day. Because of this, Coney Island was nicknamed "Nickel Empire".

Melovyye Karyery is a scenic chain of artificial lakes carved by the chalk pit quarries near the village of Krasnoselsky, Grodno where Rebecca grew up.

Operation Barbarossa

Operation Barbarossa was the name of Germany's ill-fated offensive against the Soviet Red Army in 1942. Belarus was the frontline between the two powers. According to the European Jewish Congress, some 90% of Jews in Belarus were murdered, some *in situ* and others trucked to death camps. Rebecca's family were from Grodno, a city in what is now Western Belarus. If any of her relatives survived the pogroms of the early twentieth century from which Rebecca fled and World War One, they would almost certainly have been killed during Operation Barbarossa. There is no way of knowing how or even if, she would have found this out, but one can assume that there would have been a grapevine of rumours and information, particularly as her own sons were fighting in Europe with the US army through the War.

Memorial Fountain (Bryant Park)

The Josephine Shaw Lowell Memorial Fountain is an outdoor fountain in Bryant Park, Manhattan.

Spoons

All of Rebecca's children were musical and two of her boys played spoons. Whenever the family got together, the house would erupt into a musical performance of spoons, guitar and singing.

Yennevelt

The word Yennevelt refers to the hereafter, a faraway place.

One Wandering Eye

Amblyopia is a condition also known as lazy eye, which Rebecca was known to have. Her vision worsened significantly as she grew older due to untreated diabetes.

Kussmaul breathing

Kussmaul breathing is an abnormally rapid and laboured breathing pattern which can result from certain medical conditions, such as diabetic ketoacidosis, a complication of diabetes. Rebecca died at the age of fifty four, in 1950, from diabetic complications.

Repairing the World

The literal meaning of the Hebrew word *mitzvah* is "commandment", but it has also come to mean a good deed or act of kindness or social justice to make the world better than it is (see "Tikkun Olam").

Tikkun Olam

The Hebrew phrase *tikkun olam* means "world repair." It is a Torah commandment often interpreted as engagement with social justice or doing good in order to fix or improve the world as we find it.

Physicist Erwin *Schrödinger* described how, according to the rules of quantum superposition, a cat in a box with a radioactive substance that may or may not have been released could be both dead and alive, until the box was opened and the cat's state measured.

The *Lenape* are the traditional native inhabitants of New York City. *Unami* is the Lenape's mother tongue.

General References

"Deportation of Jews from Ghetto I in Grodno, January 1943" Vad Vashim, The World Holocaust Remembrance Centre, https://www.yadvashem. org/holocaust/this-month/january/1943-3.html

Eyewitness Accounts of Anti-Jewish Persecution in Russia in the Early 20th Century: The Cowen Report - European Investigation Entry No. 9; File No. 51411/056

Fermaglich, K. (2015). „Too Long, Too Foreign ... Too Jewish": Jews, Name Changing, and Family Mobility in New York City, 1917-1942. Journal of American Ethnic History, 34(3), 34-57. doi:10.5406/ jamerethnhist.34.3.0034

Guide to the United States for the Jewish Immigrant: A Near Literal Translation of the Second Yiddish Edition (1916) by John Foster Carr, Immigrant Publication Society, https://babel.hathitrust.org/cgi/pt? id=umn.319510024691238&view=1up&seq=7

Health Conditions of Immigrant Jews on the Lower East Side of New York: 1880-1914 by Deborah Dwork, Medical History, 1981, 25: 1-40. https://pdfs.semanticscholar.org/7b13/6d59f7e4ab79f6443e4076259b 094961d244.pdf)

Liberty: The statue and the American dream (1985) by Leslie Allen

Orientation, Overview, and Omissions. In: Human Geographies Within the Pale of Settlement by Mitchell R.E.Palgrave, 2019, Macmillan, Cham. https://doi.org/10.1007/978-3-319-99145-0_1

Out of the Shtetl.* In the footsteps of Eastern European Jewish emigrants to America, 1900-1914, Gur Alroey, https://openaccess.leidenuniv.nl/bitstream/handle/1887/73038/22-01-14_ALROEY.pdf?sequence=1

Were Jews Political Refugees or Economic Migrants? Assessing the Persecution Theory of Jewish Emigration, 1881-1914, Leah Platt Boustan. http://www.econ.ucla.edu/people/papers/Boustan/Boustan387.pdf)

"Jewish Surnames Explained" Slate, Bennett Muraskin, JAN 08, 2014

A Historical Atlas of the Jewish People by Eli Barnavi, 2003

Triangle Shirtwaist: https://trianglefire.ilr.cornell.edu/primary/survivor Interviews/MaryDomskyAbrams.html

United States Holocaust Memorial Museum. "Wartime Correspondence" Jewish Perspectives on the Holocaust collection 1, https://perspectives.ushmm.org/collection/wartime-correspondence

Acknowledgements

Versions of these poems were published in The Blue Nib 'Backstory', Burrow, Live Encounters, and Hecate.

'The Lost Sister' won first prize in the November Hunter Writers Centre Writing Contest.

'Classified' won the Aug 2021 Writing contest.

'The Black Hundreds' was read aloud in the first Melbourne Jewish Book Week.

'Between the Ocean and the Stone' was featured in Raining Poetry in Adelaide 2022.

I am indebted to feedback from early readers Gillian Swain, Richard Lever, and Beth Spencer, and to Sheila Wolff, Ricky Ian Gordon, Ira Samberg, and Jeff Samberg who freely shared their memories of Rebecca (my Bobish) with me.

While I have tried to use factual information and follow the trajectory of Rebecca's migration and experiences as honestly as possible, there were many gaps in what I could find, and I have pieced the work together with other stories, histories and imaginative renderings that are quite likely to be fictive. Any mistakes or anachronistic imaginings are mine alone.

About the Author

Magdalena Ball was born in New York City, and has lived in Australia for over three decades. She is a novelist, poet, reviewer, interviewer, and is Managing Editor of Compulsive Reader. Her stories, editorials, poetry, reviews and articles have appeared in a wide number of printed anthologies and journals, and have won local and international awards. She is the author of several novels and poetry books, and runs a podcast of writer interviews called Compulsive Reader Talks.

www.ingramcontent.com/pod-product-compliance
Lightning Source LLC
Chambersburg PA
CBHW030937090426
42737CB00007B/465